T0129304

Flowing Rivers

Robert W. Barker

iUniverse, Inc.
Bloomington

Flowing Rivers

iUniverse books may be ordered through booksellers or by contacting:

iUniverse
1663 Liberty Drive
Bloomington, IN 47403
www.iuniverse.com
1-800-Authors (1-800-288-4677)

ISBN: 978-1-4759-9561-9 (sc)
ISBN: 978-1-4759-9562-6 (ebk)

Printed in the United States of America

iUniverse rev. date: 06/25/2013

To Margie,

My guide and fellow traveler.

Foreword

This small book of poetry contains fifty-two short poems written over a period of approximately one year. The poems are in the style of Japanese Tanka poetry.

I have arranged the poems in simple chronological order. Some time periods during the year were particularly difficult, when friends and close family members were battling serious illnesses. The year also encompassed the deeply disturbing massacre of innocent children at Newtown, and the Boston Marathon bombings. There were other times, however, that were filled with joy, sometimes with the simple changes of the seasons, but most prominently by the birth of my first grandchild.

Through it all, the river of my life continues to flow, and as expressed in one poem I am only now beginning to see my life unfold. May we all promise, each day, to listen and fully appreciate life's new song.

Flowing without time,
Our changing world surrounds us.
We stand, bewildered.
Walk the streets, still together;
Children, walking to the park.

April 10, 2012
Boston Time

Bright green light of spring,
Raindrops wash the newborn leaves,
Smooth, untouched by age.
Soft, hopeful, a fresh young life
Challenges the darkened day.

May 1, 2012
Spring Day

Memories return,

Short, slow drift to the island

Where my youth took flight.

Lazy geese of those past years

Have moved to other waters.

May 3, 2012
Toronto Island

Silent, I watch her,

Afraid I cannot save her.

I fear my weakness.

My strength cannot fail me now,

But age demands its tribute.

May 8, 2012
Realities

Warm wind blows softly;

Tall thin trees bend and tremble;

Their green leaves whisper.

Shy, hidden orchids greet me.

Listen! Echoes of song birds.

May 11, 2012
Wooded Retreat

In martial order,

Clouds race through the green valley;

Dry fields greet warm rain.

Ancient oaks embrace the clouds,

Then, regretful, let them go.

May 14, 2012
Afternoon Rain

Flowing together,

A touch for tomorrow's life;

Love's own arrival.

The past becomes the future

With a kiss and a blessing.

May 21, 2012
Love's Blessing

Standing on the edge,

They watch for their future life,

Embracing their love.

Belonging to all, and none,

Hope will be her own woman.

May 31, 2012
Grandfather's Dream

Her day arriving,

She faces passage, alone;

I watch, quietly.

I touch her, but I am weak;

Unwelcome tears fill my eyes.

June 12, 2012
Cynthia Prepares

Life's play is too cruel;

Short scenes of simple pleasure,

Set in painful acts.

Cast and audience of fools,

Only lights define the two.

June 16, 2012
Vigil in Boston

Quiet. I will weep.

Her trial accepts no end;

My spirit falters.

How long before the sun shines,

In this loud and fearful world?

June 21, 2012
Vigil

We will burn witches;

Driven by hot, ancient fears,

We cure them with flames.

We, the crowd, still cry for more.

Who will be tomorrow's witch?

July 13, 2012
Innocents

Listen quietly

As the rain falls on dry leaves,

And the hot, parched earth.

Dry soil drinks each noisy drop;

The river waits, patiently.

July 16, 2012
Summer Rain

She rests by the sea;
I watch three young boys swimming,
Voices bright and clear.
Waves quietly wash the rocks,
And our time quickly passes.

August 1, 2012
Ocean Interlude

Loud insect voices,

In the dark and humid night.

Frantic mating songs.

They know their time is passing;

Tomorrow is forever.

August 2, 2012
Night Song

I greet each morning,

Every change brought by the dawn.

I accept them all.

Embrace the soft new rhythms,

And the call of life's new song.

August 13, 2012
Still Singing

Sixty-seven years,

And only now beginning,

To see life unfold.

Too many years spent striving,

And far too few spent living.

August 17, 2012
Birthday

The sun, cloaked in fog,

Rises beyond tall, dark trees,

Slowly, deep orange.

For endless passing seasons

We have watched our morning sun.

September 7, 2012
Sunrise

Low, gray drifting clouds,

They caress the dark, green trees,

Wet with their blessings.

I am touched by their softness,

Across the reaches of time.

September 15, 2012
Morning

Standing, bewildered,
All life's black torrents surround
His failing body.
Earlier rejections fade,
Now shamed by larger sorrows.

September 29, 2012
Tortured Friendship

Yellow leaves falling,

Drifting through bare, black branches,

They whisper passage.

Leaves carpet the forest floor,

And greet the first frost of fall.

October 12, 2012
Fall Passage

He races the light,

And travels well-worn pathways,

Filled with dark shadows;

Passing through dark wilderness,

He hears soft voices calling.

October 23, 2012
Lonely Voices

Wind, rain, raging fire,

Destroying all vanity,

Leaving sand and bones.

Cling to the edge of the sea,

Such fierce and deadly beauty.

November 1, 2012
Storm

She shines in our eyes,

Quiet, softly insistent,

Shaping all our worlds.

The house, again so quiet,

We feel the love, still smiling.

November 12, 2012
Hope's Visit

Liquid, dark ink flows
Across life's rumpled canvas;
Brilliant white is lost.
Stretching the canvas tighter,
We paint color over black.

November 18, 2012
Living

When did we find love?

In a moment of passion,

We touched the edges.

Cautiously, we traced circles,

Afraid to test love's full strength.

November 22, 2012
Fearful of Love

Blind, I stand naked.

My body bound and useless,

Voiceless, I must wait.

Coming to me, touching me;

At last, we are together.

November 24, 2012
Waiting

Words, flowing quickly

From our lips, unsealed by time,

And kissed by friendship.

Happiness, sadness, combine,

As we turn and hurry home.

December 3, 2012
Meeting Old Friends

Grasping destiny,

Youth balance on sharp edges,

Unafraid of height.

Knowing immortality,

They face the sharp winds, and laugh.

December 12, 2012
Fearless

Children march away,

Weeping, soft innocence lost

In one sharp moment.

Can we still offer comfort?

Are we too fearful to care?

December 14, 2012
Newtown

Float over mountains;
Never will I climb again,
Not to those high peaks.
Once, I raced friends up the slopes;
Bored, I left them far behind.

December 14, 2012
Friendship Failed

Reach across the gulf,

Beyond distrust and anger,

To listen softly.

So different, so much the same.

Listen! The sound of living.

December 19, 2012
Peace Offering

Gradual fading

And loss of old connections;

All coming with age.

The season brings reminders,

But we have moved to new lands.

December 21, 2012
Christmas Cards

Our Hope consumes us;

She holds and pulls us quickly

To her destiny.

Forgive us for holding her,

And expecting her embrace.

December 22, 2012
Child

Snow falls quietly,
Faintly coating the dry grass,
Quickly dissolving.
Rain washes the palate clean;
Still, my life's colors will clash.

December 25, 2012
Dissonance

Traveling slowly,

Through the after Christmas snow,

We feel warm enough;

Cherishing the thoughts of love,

That linger from a child's smile.

December 26, 2012
Christmas Child

The face of darkness,

With fierce determination,

Assails our senses.

I refuse the growing gloom,

Intent on bright tomorrows.

January 6, 2013
Resistance

Caress life's edges,

So sharp and unforgiving;

Blood flows from fresh wounds.

All my binding skills are lost,

Useless to stop the bleeding.

January 23, 2013
Helpless

Startled, he flies swiftly,

Through the trees, to land, hidden,

Abandoning height.

Beautiful, I tell him so,

But the untouched soul is gone.

February 1, 2013
Hawk

My life has its path,

Not all that I intended,

But it is my life.

We must live what still remains,

Always seeking one more spring.

February 25, 2013
Watching for Spring

Our lives flow swiftly;

White rapids washing black rocks,

Will find peace at last.

Be still, listen quietly,

To the sounds of silent souls.

March 11, 2013
Silence

The new day, shouting,

Here I am, bright, glorious;

Let the trumpets sound.

Here I am, and my warm sun

Will melt winter's snow, at last.

March 30, 2013
Greeting Spring

The world is waiting,

Unsure, touching hopes and dreams,

Seeds of tomorrow.

I reach to grasp this moment;

Wistfully, it slips away.

April 6, 2013
Tomorrow

Dark red islands float
In an endless silver sea,
Tossed by ancient storms.
The roots of my soul are here,
Fed by the rock of my youth.

April 18, 2013
Backyard Ledge

Ghostly passages,
Two brothers, seen and unseen,
Stare at the chosen.
They sow black seeds of violence,
Swiftly growing into death.

April 19, 2013
Boston Death

Nature holds her breath;
Tall trees gather strength for spring,
With first green whispers.
Time of most abundant life,
Calls to ancient native souls.

April 22, 2013
Spring Awakening

Colored explosion,

Nature's symphony for spring,

So quickly passing.

First the quick thrill of trumpets,

Then the slow march of summer.

April 30, 2013
Spring Trees

Through endless darkness,
Blackened forests, barren lands,
Hungering for love.
Painful, ancient loss recalled,
Turn today, and kiss the sun.

May 6, 2013
Regrets Refused

Long ago we lived
Together, elbows touching;
We knew our secrets.
In deep woods, our paths diverged,
Our touch, only memory.

May 10, 2013
Reunion

She speaks with visions,
Slipping through the fog of time,
In her private world.
Confusion offers courage
To face her final passage.

May 16, 2013
Age of Confusion

Such disappointment,

Workers build a stage of steel,

Hiding lifeless stones.

We came to see a dead stage,

But still, so ancient, it breathes.

May 30, 2013
Arena at Nimes

Senses assaulted,

Brilliant marble, darkened bronze,

Spirits escaping.

Once, and still, he changed vision;

The children run, unaware.

June 1, 2013

Musée Rodin

Printed in the United States
By Bookmasters